The witnesses laid down their clothes at the feet of a young man named Saul.

Acts 7:58

Saul was a witness at the death of the first Christian martyr, Stephen, because he agreed with the killing. He guarded the clothes of the men who stoned Stephen to death.

Suddenly a light shone around him from heaven.

Acts 9:3

Saul was so eager to attack Christians that he decided to go to Damascus and arrest any that he found there. On the road he was surrounded by a heavenly light and heard the voice of Jesus asking him why he was persecuting him. He then told Saul to go into Damascus. The men with Saul could hear a voice but saw nothing. Saul fell to the ground and when he stood up he was blind, so the men led him into Damascus where he was sightless for three days, not eating or drinking during this time.

But the Lord said to him, "Go, for he is a chosen vessel of Mine to bear My name."

Acts 9:15

In Damascus a disciple, named Ananias, was told by the Lord to find Saul and put his hands upon him so he would be able to see again. Saul had been given a vision that this would happen. Ananias obeyed and Saul was able to see again. He became filled with the Holy Spirit and was then baptized.

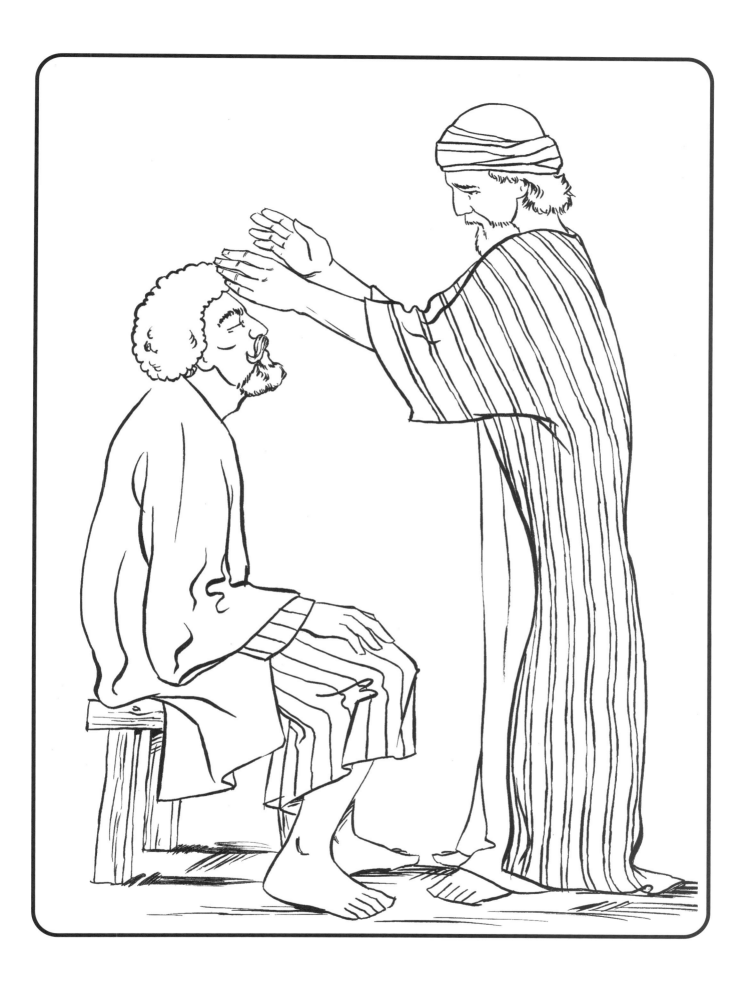

He preached the Christ in the synagogues, that He is the Son of God.

Acts 9:20

Saul now began to preach the gospel but everyone who heard him was amazed, knowing that Saul had once hated Jesus and his followers. Soon the Jews planned to kill Saul because of his preaching, so his friends lowered him over the city walls one night in a large basket and he fled to Jerusalem. The disciples there did not believe that Saul was a Christian and were afraid of him.

Then Barnabas departed for Tarsus to seek Saul.

Acts 11:25

Barnabas took Saul to the apostles and Saul told them how he had been converted when Jesus spoke to him. He then joined the apostles in preaching. Soon other people wanted to kill him for preaching the gospel and he was sent to Tarsus for safety. After a time Barnabas brought him back to Antioch, where together they served with the church and the name 'Christian' was first used.

Having fasted and prayed, and laid hands on them, they sent them away.

Acts 13:3

Saul and Barnabas were called by the Lord to preach elsewhere and Saul's name was changed to Paul. They preached in a large number of synagogues and many people were saved. The Jews were jealous of how many people listened to Paul so they opposed him. Because they rejected the word of God, Paul and Barnabas spoke to the Gentiles instead and many became believers.

BOOK 14 PAUL

13

And they were preaching the gospel there.

Acts 14:7

The two men passed through many cities preaching but always had to flee because the Jews wanted to kill them. In the city of Lystra, Paul healed a crippled man and the people worshipped him as a god. Paul was very upset at this and even though he was stoned and dragged out of the city, he returned to encourage the believers there.

He went through Syria and Cilicia, strengthening the churches.

Acts 15:41

After a time Paul wished to return to all the cities he had preached in and visit the believers there. Barnabas wanted to take John Mark with them but Paul refused because he had not helped them in their work. The two men parted and Paul travelled, strengthening the churches.

Timothy, a beloved son: Grace, mercy and peace from God the Father.

2 Timothy 1:2

In Lystra Paul met Timothy, a young believer who was highly thought of by the people there. Paul wanted to take Timothy with him and circumcised him as a disciple. Paul loved Timothy as a son and the letters he sent to him were the ones he wrote at the end of his life.

This girl followed Paul and us, and cried out.

Acts 16:17

A vision appeared to Paul one night of a man from Macedonia pleading with him to come and help them. While Paul, Timothy, Luke, Silas and others were there, a slave girl, who was possessed by a spirit that could tell the future, followed the men around, declaring that they were the servants of God. After many days Paul was annoyed and in the name of Jesus ordered the spirit to leave her. The girl was cured but her masters were very angry because they had used the spirit to make money. They dragged Paul and Silas before the authorities.

And he brought them out and said, "Sirs, what must I do to be saved?"

Acts 16:30

In Philippi, a city in Macedonia, Paul and Silas were beaten and thrown in jail. That night, as they prayed, there was a great earthquake and all the doors were opened and the chains were loosened. The jailer was frightened but Paul told him to believe in the Lord. This jailer took them to his home where he and his family were baptized. The next morning the authorities learnt that Paul was a Roman and asked him to leave. He left after he had encouraged the believers.

All who dwelt in Asia heard the word of the Lord Jesus, both Jews and Greeks.

Acts 19:10

In Ephesus, Paul came across some disciples who had been baptized by John but did not know of the Holy Spirit. Paul placed his hands on them and the men, about twelve in all, received the Holy Spirit. God used Paul in such a way that even handkerchiefs and aprons that touched his body could heal the sick. Through this the message and the power of the gospel spread.

"Now I ...am judged for the hope of the promise made by God to our fathers."

Acts 26:6

Paul continued travelling, preaching and healing. He was arrested and often beaten, but he never lost his love for God. Many men wanted to kill him and he spent much time in chains. He wrote letters to the churches while in prison and these are found in the New Testament. He had to defend himself before different rulers.

"Unless these men stay in the ship, you cannot be saved."

Acts 27:31

Paul and some other prisoners were sent on a ship to Rome but there was a storm. An angel of God promised Paul that no one on the ship would die and he encouraged the men. They were still concerned, especially when the food ran out, but they all made it safely to land.

For to me, to live is Christ, and to die is gain.

Philippians 1:21

Paul was the greatest missionary, suffering deeply for the gospel, as God had intended, and spending much of his life in prison. Many of his friends deserted him and he became very ill but he never stopped praying and worshipping. He was finally executed for his faith but God used him wonderfully during his life.

Also in this series

THE PARABLES. Jesus often taught with parables, which were stories that taught lessons about God. Many people did not understand what he was saying so he sometimes explained them. They make it easier for us to understand what God is like and how much he loves us.

Find out more in Book 15